A Few Words On The Arabic Derivatives In Hindustani: Their Formation And Application To The Above Language

L. Benson

In the interest of creating a more extensive selection of rare historical book reprints, we have chosen to reproduce this title even though it may possibly have occasional imperfections such as missing and blurred pages, missing text, poor pictures, markings, dark backgrounds and other reproduction issues beyond our control. Because this work is culturally important, we have made it available as a part of our commitment to protecting, preserving and promoting the world's literature. Thank you for your understanding.

A

FEW WORDS

ON THE

ARABIC DERIVATIVES

IN

HINDŪSTĀNĪ;

THEIR FORMATION AND APPLICATION TO THE ABOVE LANGUAGE;
BEING AN EASY METHOD OF ACQUIRING A VAST NUMBER
OF USEFUL HINDŪSTĀNĪ WORDS.

BY

LIEUT<sup>T.</sup> BENSON,

MADRAS ARMY.

LONDON:
JAMES MADDEN; 8, LEADENHALL STREET.

MDCCCLII.

## PREFACE.

These pages were originally arranged for practise in the Hindūstānī language, during my leave in England; but, at the suggestion of some friends, their publication has been undertaken, with the hope that they may prove of some advantage to the student in Hindūstānī; not so much so, however, to the entire beginner, as to one who has already overcome the first rudiments.

Hindūstānī being a combination of languages, and Arabic words or derivatives forming a considerable portion thereof, I have attempted to elucidate the formation of these derivatives in as simple a manner as possible, avoiding all unnecessary detail of the various anomalies which occur in Arabic, caused by the vowel points, as they tend, I think, in some measure to obstruct the path of the student.

The principal advantages which I hope may be derived from the perusal of these pages are—first, that of learning the method of forming from one word or root some twenty or thirty useful Arabic derivatives, which are copiously blended with Hindūstānī: secondly, of acquiring a critical knowledge, and, at the same time, a correctness in the orthography of these words, which will greatly assist the student in translating, either from the Hindūstānī or English.

In the few sentences which I have given by way of examples, I have endeavoured to introduce as many Arabic derivatives as I deemed propriety would admit; but should I, in doing so, have gone beyond the bounds of the Hindūstānī idiom, I trust this, as well as other defects or errors which may occur, will be indulgently passed over.

*August*, 1852.

# CONTENTS.

## CHAPTER I.

                                                                     PAGE.

THE REGULAR TRILITERAL VERBS—
    Active and Passive, with their Derivatives, etc...... 1

## CHAPTER II.

IRREGULAR VERBS .................................................. 21
    Concave .................................................. 23
    Similar ................................................... 25
    Defective, etc............................................ 26

NOUNS of Time........................................................ 27
    „   Place ................................................. *ib.*
    „   Instrument ............................................ 28

NUMBERS................................................................ 30

COMPARISON .......................................................... 31

# ABBREVIATIONS.

| | | |
|---|---|---|
| *s.* | for | Substantive. |
| *m.* | ,, | Masculine. |
| *f.* | ,, | Feminine. |
| *v.* | ,, | Verb. |
| *a.* | ,, | Active. |
| *p.* | ,, | Passive. |
| *n.* | ,, | Neuter. |
| *c.* | ,, | Causal. |
| *adj.* | ,, | Adjective. |
| *part.* | ,, | Participle. |
| *fr.* | ,, | From. |
| *r.* | ,, | Root. |

# ARABIC DERIVATIVES
## IN
# HINDŪSTĀNĪ.

---

THE Arabic derivatives which are used in Hindjūstānī are formed from the roots of the Arabic verbs. These verbs are divided into what is termed triliteral (ثلاثي), quadriliteral (رباعي), simile (مثال), concave (اجوف), defective (ناقص), and hamzated (مهموز). The triliteral verb in Arabic is very simple in the formation of its several conjugations, and, being of the utmost importance in Hindūstānī, it will be chiefly and primarily considered. As the derivatives of the quadriliteral verb are seldom or ever met with in Hindūstānī, they are entirely omitted. The concave, simile, and defective verbs, etc., being subject to various permutations and inflections, caused by the vowel points *fatha* ( ́), *kasra* ( ̣), and *damna* (ʼ), will be partially explained hereafter.

The triliteral, or regularly conjugated three-lettered verb, has three consonants in its radical form, as—نصر, عمد, فتح, قصد, علم, etc. It has thirteen conjugations, each having a preterite (which is always the root), imperative, and future tense; with a participle, and infinitive or verbal noun, both active and passive (*vide* page 33). The preterites, participles, and infinitives or verbal nouns, being all that are required here for the formation of the derivatives used in Hindūstānī, the other tenses are omitted; and likewise, for the same reason, the ninth, eleventh, twelfth, and thirteenth conjugations.

### ACTIVE VOICE.

| Infinitive or Verbal Noun. | Participle. | Preterite. | |
|---|---|---|---|
| قصداً | قاصد | قصد | 1 |
| تقصید | مُقصد | قصد | 2 |
| مقاصدت | مقاصد | قاصد | 3 |
| اقصاد | مقصد | اقصد | 4 |
| تقصد | متقصد | تقصد | 5 |
| تقاصد | متقاصد | تقاصد | 6 |
| انقصاد | منقصد | انقصد | 7 |
| اقتصاد | مقتصد | اقتصد | 8 |
| استقصاد | مستقصد | استقصد | 10 |

### PASSIVE VOICE.

| Participle. | |
|---|---|
| مقصد | 2 |
| مُقصد | 4 |
| مستقصد | 10 |
| مقصود | 13 |

The above participles are all that are necessary to be given, as they are the only part of the passive voice commonly met with in Hindūstānī. In formation they resemble the participles of the same conjugations in the active voice. The above forms, it will be noticed, are merely the roots increased by certain letters, and these letters are either ي (yē), ت (tē), س (sīn), م (mīm), ن nūn, و (wāw), or ا (alif); and the above letters, when combined, form the Arabic word يتسمنوا, which translated, signifies 'they fatten,' and are termed (حرف الزواد) extra letters or characteristics. The participle active of the first conjugation, takes (ا) alif after the first radical letter—as قاصد, 'a messenger.' The participles, both active and passive, are used in Hindūstānī as adjectives, and also in a substantive sense—as قاتل 'a murderer;' محمد, 'praised,' 'the Prophet Mahomed.' And again, to these participles, or to any of the verbal derivatives, the Hindustani verbs ركهنا, اٹهانا, كرنا, پانا, هونا, etc., are affixed. There seems to be no rule for determining how, or to what particular derivatives, these verbs are to be affixed; they are combined indiscriminately, and are used as active, passive, and neuter verbs. The infinitive of this conjugation, has ا (alif) with *tanvīn* ( ً ) or nunation over it, and it is a common form of adverb in Hindūstānī. With a view to illustrate the sense in which these derivatives are applied in Hindūstānī, I shall give a few examples, and short sentences.

*Examples of the First Conjugation.*

ADVERBS.

عمداً, 'intentionally.'   ضرباً, 'violently.'
عقلاً, 'wisely,' 'prudently.'   قهراً, 'forcibly.'
جبراً, 'forcibly,' 'violently.'   سهواً, 'erroneously.'
قبلاً, 'formerly,' 'previously.'   قصداً, 'designedly.'
شرعاً, 'lawfully.'

## PARTICIPLES, ADJECTIVES, AND SUBSTANTIVES.

قاتل, 'killing.' s.m. 'murderer.' adj. 'fatal.'

قاصر, adj. 'deficient,' 'failing.'

لازم, adj. 'necessary,' 'requisite.'

قابل, 'receiving.' adj. 'clever,' 'fit.'

فاضل, adj. 'virtuous,' 'learned.'

حاصل, s.m. 'profit,' 'gain,' 'acquiring.'

فاتح, s.m. 'assistant,' 'defender.'

مالک, s.m. 'a king, 'owner.'

حاکم, s.m. 'a judge.' adj. 'liberal.'

حادث, adj. 'new,' 'appearing.'

حافظ, s.m. 'a guardian.'

حاکم, s.m. 'ruler,' 'commander.'

## VERBS.

قتل کرنا, v.a. 'to slay, kill.'

نفع پانا, v.n. 'to gain profit.'

قصد رکهنا, v.n. 'to project,' 'to proceed as on a journey.'

حکم دینا, v.a. 'to order.'

درج کرنا, v.a. 'to copy, write.'

رفع هونا or کرنا, v.p., v.a. 'to remove or be removed.'

لاحق هونا, v.p. 'to be overreached.'

حاصل کرنا, v.a. 'to accomplish, obtain.'

فارغ هونا, v.p. 'to be free,' 'to be at ease.'

دفع هونا or کرنا, v.p. 'to be turned back.' v.a. 'to ward off.'

دعا مانگنا, v.n. 'to ask a blessing.'

قسم دلانا, v.a. 'to administer an oath.'

قسم کهانا, v.n. 'to swear.'

قرض رکهنا or لینا, v.n. 'to owe,' 'to borrow.'

خارج کرنا, v.a. 'to expel.'

قابل هونا, v.p. 'to deserve.' 'to merit.'

| | |
|---|---|
| حاصر هونا, v.p. 'to be present.' | غالب هونا, v.p. 'to be victorious.' |
| لازم هونا, v.p. 'to be necessary, incumbent on.' | قاصر هونا, v.p. 'to be deficient.' |
| | رقم کرنا, v.a. 'to write.' |
| فاضل هونا, v.p. 'to be learned, virtuous, excellent.' | |

And again we have another form of derivatives, ending in ه and ت; and, as a general rule in Arabic, all words ending in ت are feminine, and those in ه are masculine, with some exceptions: as—خادم, 'a slave,' 'servant;' خادمه, 'a female servant,' 'slave,' etc.

| | |
|---|---|
| حرمت, s.f. 'chastity,' 'dignity,' 'character.' | صرفه, s.f. 'expense,' 'profusion.' |
| حرکت, s.f. 'motion,' 'action,' 'interruption.' | قصه, s.m. 'tale,' 'story.' |
| حرفت, s.f. 'trade,' 'profession.' | لطمه, s.m. 'slap,' 'blow.' |
| عصمت, s.f. 'continence,' 'honor.' | نقطه, s.m. 'a point,' 'dot.' |
| قدرت, s.f. 'power,' 'authority.' | نقشه, s.m. 'portrait,' 'map,' 'plan.' |
| قسمت, s.f. 'fate,' 'fortune,' 'lot.' | باصره, s.m. 'sight,' 'the sense of seeing.' |
| نزهت, s.f. 'delight,' 'freshness,' 'integrity.' | باکره, s.f. 'a virgin.' |
| نسبت, s.f. 'relation,' 'affinity,' 'reference.' | حادثه, s.m. 'incident,' 'event.' |
| نصرت, s.f. 'victory.' | حامله, s.f. 'pregnant.' |
| | خاتمه, s.m. 'conclusion,' 'final.' |
| | صاحبه, s.f. 'lady,' 'mistress.' |
| | عارضه, s.m. 'an accident,' 'an event.' |

کلفت, s.f. 'trouble,' 'vexation.'
فاحشه, s.f. 'a harlot.'
فاسده, adj. 'noxious,' 'bad.'
خطبه, s.m. 'A sermon,' 'oration.'
فاصله, s.m. 'a space,' 'distance.'
خطره, s.m. 'fear,' 'risk,' 'danger.'
قاعده, s.m. 'basis,' 'the rules of grammar.'
رقعه, s.m. 'note,' 'epistle.'
قافله, s.m. 'a body of travellers,' 'a caravan.'
صدمه, s.m. 'blow,' 'calamity.'
صدقه, s.m. 'alms,' 'offerings.'

These derivatives sometimes end in ی (*vide* page 29), in which case they are, in general, feminine nouns, or adjectives; for, in Arabic, adjectives,* as well as nouns, have masculine and feminine genders, as:

بدلی, s.f. 'relief of watches,' 'exchange of sentries.'
عاجزی, s.f. 'poverty,' 'weakness.'
عرضی, s.f. 'a petition,' 'memorial.'
ظاهری, adj. 'apparent.'
نقدی, adj., 'monied,' 'relating to money.'
غرقی, s.f. 'flooding of lands,' 'inundation.'
صاحبی, s.f. 'lordship.'
قلبی, adj. 'hearty,' 'cordial.'
حاکمی, s.f. 'government,' 'rule.'
نقلی, s.m. 'a narrator.' adj. 'copied.'
حاضری, s.f. 'breakfast.'
عاشقی, s.f. 'making love,' 'courtship.'

---

* The Arabic grammarians do not consider adjectives as differing from nouns as parts of speech.

The participle with nunated alif ( ا ) is sometimes, but rarely, met with as an adverb, as: ظاهراً, 'publicly,' 'apparently.'

جنرل صاحب جانتي هين فدوي سي ايسي تقصير قصداً نه هوي

'The General is aware that the petitioner (your slave) never intentionally committed such a fault.'

پادشاه کا وزیرِ عالي نهایت قابل و فاضل تها

'The King's Prime Minister was most efficient and excellent.'

يروديس پادشاه ني يوحنا کي بهائي يعقوب کو تلوار سي قتل و جدل کيا

'Herod the king slew James, the brother of John, with the sword.'

The infinitive or verbal noun of the second conjugation has ت and ي for its extra letters. It is invariably a feminine noun in Hindūstānī, and used sometimes adverbially. The participle has م, which is the first characteristic of this, as also of all the conjugations, with the exception of the first.

*Examples of the Second Conjugation.*

VERBAL NOUNS.

تکریم, s.f. 'respect.'  
تکبیر, s.f. 'pride.'  
تفریق, s.f. 'separation,' 'division.'

تعریف, s.f. 'praise.'
تعظیم, s.f. 'honor.'
تعجیل, s.f. 'haste,' 'expedition.'
تعلیم, s.f. 'instruction,' 'tuition.'
تفہیم, s.f. 'teaching,' 'informing.'
تقلید, s.f. 'forgery,' 'imitation.'
تقدیر, s.f. 'fate,' 'destiny.'
تکلیف, s.f. 'difficulty,' 'trouble.'

### VERBS.

تکفین کرنا, v.a. 'to bury,' 'to coffin.'
تقریر کرنا, v.a. 'to relate, detail.'
تعمیر کرنا or ہونا, v.p. and v.a. 'to erect,' 'to be built.'
تحریر ہونا, v.p. 'to be written.'
تخفیف دینا or کرنا, v.a. 'to remit, mitigate.'
تنقیح کرنا, v.a. 'to search, investigate.'

### PARTICIPLES AND ADJECTIVES.

مبشر, s.m. 'a bearer of glad tidings,' 'an evangelist.'
محرر, s.m. 'a writer.'
محرک, adj. 'moving,' v. 'causing to move.'
مدرس, s.m. 'a teacher, professor.'
محرم, adj. 'sacred,' 'first Mahomedan month.'
محصل, adj. 'gathering,' s.m. 'a dun, tax-gatherer.'
مخبر, s.m. 'a counsellor,' adj. 'prudent.'
منجم, s.m. 'an astronomer, astrologer.'

### VERBS.

مکبر ہونا, v.p. 'to be proud,' etc.
مدبر ہونا, v.p. 'to be prudent,' etc.

### ADVERB.

تحقيقاً, adv. 'certainly,' 'truly.'

جب نايك كي شجاعت كي خبر ٹپو سلطان بہادر
كي سماعت مين آئي تب اسني بڑي تعظيم و تعريف
ديكر اسكو سرفراز كيا

'Tippoo Sultān, on ascertaining intelligence of the naik's (corporal's) gallant conduct, praised him greatly, and promoted him.'

تحقيقاً جو كوي نيك نوكري و نمك حلالي كري تو
مكرم هوئنگي

'Verily, whoever performs faithful service, will be respected.'

The extra letters of the third conjugation being م and آ, we have the following examples:—

### INFINITIVES OR VERBAL NOUNS.

مدافعت, s.f. 'repulsion,' 'driving back.'  
محاربت, s.f. 'battle,' 'engagement.'

مداخلت, s.f. 'intrusion,' 'intermeddling.'  
محاصرت, s.f. 'protection,' 'succour.'

مقاربت, s.f. 'connection,' 'friendship.'  
محافظت, s.f. 'aid,' 'assistance.'

مقاتله, s.m. 'slaughter,' 'battle.'  
مخالفت, s.f. 'mixing together in society.'

ملاحظه, s.m. 'inspection,' 'consideration.'  
مجالست, s.f. 'assembly,' 'congregation.'

## PARTICIPLES AND ADJECTIVES.

ملازم, adj. 'attentive.' part. 'attendant.'

مکاتب, adj. 'corresponding.' part. 'correspondent.'

مناسب, adj. 'fit,' 'proper.'

مصاحب, part. 'companion,' 'friend.'

ممانع, adj. 'prohibiting.'

منازع, adj. 'contesting.'

## VERBS.

ملاحظه کرنا, v.a. 'to regard, inspect.'

مصالحه کرنا, v.a. 'to compound, compromise.'

مصالح ڈالنا, v.a. 'to season (with spices).'

مقابل هونا, v.p. 'to be opposed to,' 'to be drawn out in battle array.'

مطالعه کرنا, v.a. 'to study, peruse.'

مصاحب هونا, v.p. 'to be in communion.'

مخالفان اپني جاسوسيون سي يه کيفيت معلوم کر بتعجيل تمام قلعي کي محافضت و محارست کي خاطر بڑي بڑي مورچي باند هني لگي

'The enemy, on obtaining this information from their spies, commenced preparing heavy batteries to protect the fort.'

The extra letters of the infinitive of the fourth conjugation are two alifs (ا): this form, with a few exceptions, is a masculine noun. The plural form of some (*vide* page 31) Arabic substantives are similar to this verbal noun; but they can be easily distinguished by the sense in which they are used.

## Examples of the Fourth Conjugation.

#### INFINITIVES AND VERBAL NOUNS.

اجماع, s.m. 'assembly,' 'council.'

ادراج, s.m. 'insertion,' 'folding together.'

اجمال, s.m. 'compendious abstract.'

اشراك, s.m. 'participating,' 'partnership.'

اخراج, s.m. 'evacuation,' 'expulsion.'

اعمال, s.m. 'causing to act.'

اعراض, s.m. 'averseness,' 'dislike.'

#### PARTICIPLES AND ADJECTIVES.

##### Extra Letter—م

مبطل, part. 'abolisher,' 'annihilating.'

مخبر, part. 'informer,' 'announcing news.'

مجمل, part. 'contracted,' 'abridged.'

مخلص, adj. 'pure.' part. 'sincere friend.'

محسن, adj. 'chaste,' 'continent.'

ممکن, adj. 'possible,' 'accessibility.'

اجمالی, adj. 'abridged,' 'compendious.'

مجملاً, adv. 'in short,' 'summarily.'

#### VERBS.

الزام هونا, v.a. 'to be convinced, confuted.'

انکار کرنا, v.a. 'to deny, refuse.'

انصاف لینا or کرنا, v.a. 'to seek justice,' 'to administer justice.'

انعام دینا, v.a. 'to bestow favours, gifts, etc.'

ممکن هونا, v.p. 'to be possible.'

ملهم هونا, v.p. 'to be inspired.'

لشکر کي مفسدون کي دلون مين آتشِ فساد بهرکني لگي

'The seditious troops of the army began to exhibit a spirit of mutiny.'

اسني سفر کرني کا ارادہ رکھا

'He determined to set out on a journey.'

انصاف پانا کچھو ممکن هي غیر

'It is impossible to get redress.'

*Examples of the Fifth Conjugation.*

Extra Letter—ت.

#### VERBAL NOUNS.

تحکم, s.m. 'authority,' 'government.'

تصرف, s.m. 'profusion,' 'extravagance.'

تحرم, s.m. 'pity,' 'compassion.'

تعلق, s.m. 'connexion.' 'manor,' 'lordship.' 'estate.'

تجسس, s.m. 'investigation,' 'exploring.'

تعهد, s.m. 'an agreement,' 'engagement.'

ترصد, s.m. 'expectation,' 'hope.'

تملق, s.m. 'flattery,' 'cajoling.'

#### VERBS.

تملق کرنا, v.a. 'to flatter.'

تلطف کرنا, v.a. 'to oblige, show favor or kindness.'

تصرف کرنا, v.a. 'to expend extravagantly.'

تلفظ کرنا, v.a. 'to pronounce.'

## PARTICIPLES AND ADJECTIVES.

Extra Letters—ت, م.

متفكر, adj. 'pensive,' 'thoughtful.'
متبدل, adj. 'changing,' 'alternate.'
متفق, adj. 'separate,' 'distinct.'

مترحم, adj. 'merciful,' 'pitying.'
متتبع, part. 'imitator.'
متجسس, part. 'spy.'

### VERBS.

متعلق هونا, v.p. 'to be dependant.'
متعجب هونا, v.p. 'to be astonished, full of admiration.'

متفرق هونا, v.p. 'to be separated, dispersed.'
متفكر هونا, v.p. 'to be thoughtful, pensive.'

اپني تمام مال تصرف مين لاكر متفكر هوا
'He was sorrowful at having squandered all his property.'

### Examples of the Sixth Conjugation.

Extra Letters—آ, ت.

#### VERBAL NOUNS OR INFINITIVES.

تقارب, s.m. 'approaching one another.'
تقابل, s.m. 'encountering opposition.'

تشابه, s.m. 'similitude,' 'resemblance.'
تعداد, s.m. 'computation.'

### VERBS.

تغافل هونا, v.p. 'to be negligent,' 'careless.'
تدارك كرنا, v.a. 'to make reparation, redress.'

14

تجاهل هونا, v.p. 'to be ignorant, apathetic.'
تلاش كرنا, v.a. 'to search, seek.'

متزايد هونا, v.p. 'to be increased.'
متلاطم هونا, v.p. 'to be dashed by the waves.'

PARTICIPLES AND ADJECTIVES.

Extra Letters—م, ت, آ.

متظالم, part. 'oppressing.'
متعارف, adj. 'known.'

متراكم, part. 'accumulating.' adj. 'collected.'
متعاقب, adj. 'following,' 'successive.'

متشابه, s.m. 'a simile,' 'metaphor.'

In Arabic the conjugations have different significations. Thus the first, second, and fourth, have an active or neuter sense; the third and sixth imply ~~neutrality~~ *mutuality*; the fifth, seventh, and eighth, are used passively; and the tenth signifies a desire of, a request for.

When it occurs that the letters of the root are the same as the characteristics or serviles, the two similar letters coalesce and take *tashdīd* (ّ); as, in the sixth conjugation, if the radical be a ت or ط, then تتمام becomes تمّام: and, again, the characteristic ن of the seventh conjugation takes *tashdīd* (ّ), as انكار becomes انّكار. In like manner, sometimes, م, when a radical, becomes ن with the *tashdīd*; and, also, in the eighth conjugation, if the radical be either a ص or ض, the servile ت becomes ط—as اضتراب becomes اضطراب; and, if ذ or د, the اضترار becomes اضطرار, and characteristic ت, in the first instance, becomes د—as ائتاد becomes ائداد ; and, secondly, the ت coalesces with the د, and takes *tashdid*—as, ادتغام becomes ادّغام.

*Examples of the Seventh Conjugation.*

Extra Letters—ا, ان.

### VERBAL NOUNS OR INFINITIVES.

اندراج, s.m. 'being folded together.'
انصرام, s.m. 'accomplishment,' 'finishing.'
اندفاع, s.m. 'repulsion,' 'prohibited.'
انقسام, s.m. 'division,' 'partition.'
انقطاع, s.m. 'being cut off,' 'failure.'
انقاص, s.m. 'contraction,' 'constipation.'

### VERBS.

منقطع کرنا or هونا, v.a. 'to cut off.' v.p. 'to be finished.'
انفصال کرنا, v.a. 'to decide, settle.'
منفعت or متفع هونا, v.p. 'to gain profit, advantage.'
انحراف کرنا, v.a. 'to turn aside, apostatize.'
منعدم هونا, v.p. 'to be annihilated.'
انحصار کرنا, v.a. 'to surround, besiege.'
منجمد هونا, v.p. 'to be congealed, frozen.'
انبساط هونا, v.p. 'to be glad, happy.'

### ADJECTIVES AND PARTICIPLES.

Extra Letters—م, ن.

منقتل, adj. 'slain,' 'killed.'
منفرج, adj. 'open,' 'separate,' 'happy.'
منکشف, adj. 'discovered,' 'revealed.'
منفسد, adj. 'corrupted.' part. 'seditious, rebellious person.'

انفصالِ کڑٹ

سرداران کڑٹ قیدی کو تقصیرمند پاکی یوں فتویٰ دیتی ہیں

'DECISION OF THE COURT.'

'The members of the court having found the prisoner guilty, sentence him as follows.'

سوداگران خرید و فروخت سی بہت سی منفعت پاتی ہیں

'The merchants reap great profit from trading.'

*Examples of the Eight Conjugation.*

Extra Letters—ا, ات.

### VERBAL NOUNS OR INFINITIVES.

اعتماد, s.m. 'faith,' 'trust.'
اعتقاد, s.m. 'faith,' 'confidence.'
اعتزال, s.m. 'secession,' 'dissenting.'
اعتبار, s.m. } 'trustworthy,
اعتباری, s.f. } confidence.'
اعتدال, s.m. 'rectitude,' 'evenness.'
اعتراض, s.m. } 'discussion,'
اعتراضی, s.f. } 'objection.'

### ADVERB.

احتیاطاً, adv. 'cautiously.'

### ADJECTIVES AND PARTICIPLES.

منتقل, adj. 'transported.'
مشترک, part. 'partner,' adj. 'common.'
ممتحن, adj. 'examining.' part. 'examiner.'
منتقش, adj. 'painted,' 'engraved.'

## VERBS.

انتظار کرنا, v.a. 'to expect, look out for.'
اعتراف کرنا, v.a. 'to confess.'

مستمل هونا, v.p. 'to comprise,' 'contain.'
مختصر هونا, v.p. 'to be abridged.'

### Examples of the Tenth Conjugation.

#### VERBAL NOUNS OR INFINITIVES.

استخلاص, s.m. 'seeking to liberate,' 'pure,' 'free.'
استقلال, s.m. 'resolution,' 'absolute.'
استفهام, s.m. 'desire of information.'

استمداد, s.f. 'desiring assistance, aid.'
استکمال, s.m. 'completion,' 'seeking perfection.'
استهلاک, s.m. 'seeking destruction, suicide.'

#### ADJECTIVES AND PARTICIPLES.

مستغفر, adj. 'asking pardon,' 'craving forgiveness.'
مستفس, adj. 'seeking explanation, interpretation.'

مستعمل, adj. 'accustomed,' 'practised.'
مستقبل, s.m. 'future tense.'

#### VERBS.

استعمال کرنا, v.a. 'to use.'
استقلالی کرنا, v.n. 'to determine,' 'to be resolute.'

مستغرق هونا, v.p. 'to be immersed, drowned.'
مستظهر هونا, v.p. 'to be supported, aided.'

سرکارِ سکه ناخنِ انتقام سی عقدِ صلاح کو کهولکی

انگریز سی جنگ و جدل کرنی کی اِرادی سی پنجاب کی ندی پار ہوئی اور لرڈ گاف بہادر یہ حقیقت معلوم کرکی بلاتوقف فروزپور میں متعین تھی سو فوج کی استعانت و استمداد کی خاطر کئی رجمنٹ روانہ کر اپ خود تمام فوج زیرِ حکم لی تشریفت لی ائی اور مخالفوں [مخالفوں] کی قریب آ رخت اقامت کا ڈالی اور جب دونوں فوج مقابلہ ہوی تب انگریزی سپاہ کی دلوں میں اشتعالِ جوانمردی مشتعل و ملتہب ہو سکھ کی مستحکم جایوں پر سخت حملہ کئی

'The Sikh government having revengefully broken the treaty of peace with the British, crossed the Punjab river with hostile intentions. Lord Gough, on hearing this intelligence, quickly dispatched succour to the force stationed at Ferozpore; and, placing himself at the head of the army, marched on the enemy, and encamped in their vicinity. When the two armies confronted each other, the British soldiers, impelled by the spirit of bravery, vigorously attacked the strong intrenchments of the Sikhs,' etc.

مدرس میں جمع ہوکر معطل رہاتھا سو جنرال کورٹ مارشل کی روبرو نیچی لکھا جاتا سو دعوی پر فلانی رجمنٹ کی سپاہی کی حریف ہوی دریافت

'At a General Court-Martial held at Madras, and continued by adjournment, a private of one of the regiments was arraigned on the following charge.'

مین رجمنٹ کو رضا کي موافق متوجہ ہوکر راماپٹن تک پهنچا اور وهان کي مسجد مین دو شخص حیدرآبادي میري شریک ہوي

'At the expiration of my leave I set out to rejoin my regiment, and, on my arrival at Rāmāpatam, in the temple of that place, I became acquainted with two men, natives of Hyderābād.'

### PASSIVE VOICE.

The passive participles (with the exception of the form مقصود) are similar in formation to those of the active voice. The past passive participle has م and و for its extra letters, as—معلوم from علم.

معقول, adj. 'reasonable,' 'proper.' معقولہ, s.m.

معشوقہ, s.f. 'mistress.'
معشوق, adj. 'beloved.'

مذکور, adj. 'related,' 'above-mentioned.'

مشہود, adj. 'proved,' 'attested.'

معروف, adj. 'noted,' 'celebrated.'

معمولي, s.f. 'customary,' 'practised.'

مشغولہ, s.m. 'employment,' 'occupation.'

مشکوري, s.f. 'reward,' 'thanking.'

The feminine noun is formed by affixing the ت to the form معقولي (*vide* page 6), as—

معقوليت, s.f. 'reasonableness' مظلوميت, s.f. 'oppression,'
معزوليت, 'tyranny.'
معصوميت, s.f. 'innocence,' 'simplicity.'

### VERBS.

محروم کرنا, v.a. 'to exclude, prohibit.'

محفوظ هونا, v.p. 'to be protected, preserved.'

مقتول هونا, v.p. 'to restrain, kill.'

مجروح هونا, v.p. 'to be wounded.'

## CHAPTER II.

### IRREGULAR VERBS.

Verbal roots of the form مد, عز, حق, etc., are, with a few imperfections, regularly conjugated. The imperfections consist in contraction, or dropping their final radical and taking *tashdīd* (ّ), as عزّت, s.f. 'grandeur,' 'power,' for عززت; and مدّت, s.f. 'length of time,' for مددت. The first, third, fourth, sixth, seventh, eighth, and tenth conjugations, admit of contraction. Derivative forms of the third, sixth, seventh, and eighth conjugations, are of too rare occurrence in Hindūstānī to require examples.

| CONJ. | VERBAL NOUNS. | PARTICIPLES, ETC. |
|---|---|---|
| 1st. | غصّه, s.m. 'anger;' for غصصه. | عاقّ, adj. 'disobedient;' for عاقق. |
| 2nd. | تجديد, s.f. 'renewal,' 'novelty;' from جدّ. | محقّق, adj. 'authenticated;' from حقّ. |
| ,, | تميم, s.f. 'completion;' from تمّ. | مخطّط, adj. 'incipient beard of youth;' from خطّ. |
| 4th. | امداد, s.f. 'assistance,' 'help;' from مدّ. | مخلّ, part. 'disturber;' for مخلل. |

5th. تجسس, s.m. 'spying,' 'investigating;' from جس.

متقرر, adj. 'established,' 'fixed;' from قر.

10th. استمرار, s.m. 'continuation,' 'perseverance;' from مر.

مسجب, adj. 'desirable;' for مسجبب.

„ استمداد, s.m. 'desiring help, assistance, aid;' from مد.

مستقل, adj. 'firm;' for مستقلل.

PASSIVE VOICE.

مخصوص, past part. 'particular;' from خص. The passive bears similar contractions to the active voice.

I do not intend entering into a full explanation of the rules which cause the many permutations of the irregular verbs; but shall endeavour to exemplify them sufficiently by a few examples, to enable a beginner to distinguish them in Hindūstānī and become acquainted with their formations. All the inflections of the imperfect verbs are caused by the vowels فتحة *fatha* ( ́), كسرة *kasra* ( ̗), ضمة *damna* ( ́), and moveable *alif* or همزة *hamzah* ( ̛). When the vowels *fatha*, *kasra*, and *damna*, are expressed thus, with ا (*alif*), و (*wāw*), ي (*ye*), these letters are said to have their similar or natural vowels; when differently written, as أ, و, ي, these letters have their dissimilar vowels. Verbs having و or ي for their second radical are termed hollow verbs (اجوف), and they partake of greater irregularities than any other class of imperfect verbs. The hollow verbs, as قَوَلَ and قَيَدَ, have their dissimilar vowel *fatha*, and, according to the Arabic rules of the permutations of و and ي, these letters, if preceded by or expressed with their dissimilar vowel *fatha*, become *alif*, as قَوَلَ becomes قَالَ, and قَيَدَ becomes قَادَ; and again, in the participle active, the و having *kasra* becomes ي, and قَاوِل becomes قَايِل. The irregular conjugations of the hollow verbs are the fourth, seventh, eighth, and tenth.

*Examples of the Concave Verbs.*

VERBAL NOUNS OR INFINITIVES.　　PARTICIPLES.

عور or عورت, s.f. 'women,' 'wife.'　　سایر, adj. 'walking;' from سیر.

افاقت, s.f. or افاقه, s.m. 'convalescence;' from فوق.　　قایم, adj. 'fixed,' 'stable,' 'firm;' from قوم.

اقامت, s.f. 'dwelling,' 'abode;' from قوم.　　مطیع, adj. 'submissive,' 'obedient;' from طوع.

انقیاد, s.m. 'obedience,' 'submission;' from قید.　　مضاف, adj. 'annexed;' from ضیف.

انقیال, s.m. 'promise,' 'consent;' from قول.　　منقال, adj. 'speaking;' from قول.

امتیاز, s.m. 'discrimination,' 'discretion;' from میز.　　مشتاق, adj. 'desirous;' from شوق.

احتیاج, s.m. 'necessary wants;' from حوج.　　محتاج, adj. 'poor,' 'indigent;' from حوج.

اختیار, s.m. 'choice,' 'option;' from خیر.
مختار, adj. 'elected,' 'absolute;' from خیر.

استراحت, s.f. 'ease,' 'repose;' from روح.
مستقیم, adj. 'right,' 'straight;' from قوم.

استفاده, s.m. 'profit,' 'advantage;' from فید.
مستفاد or مستفید, adj. 'profitable;' from فید.

With the exception of the past participle, the passive voice is susceptible of the same changes as the active. In the passive participle the radical و* is thrown out, and, for ملووث, ملوث, 'polluted,' is written; and ملووم makes ملوم, 'reproached,' 'blamed.'

مهموز, or Hamzated verbs—which have moveable *alif* for one of their radicals, as طفا, سال, اثر—are nearly similar in their conjugations to the regular verbs. The participle active, in consequence of having the two *alifs* meeting, the *hamza* is thrown out and the remaining *alif* is pronounced long, taking *maddah* (مده)—as, اائر becomes آثر. And, in the participle fourth, *alif*, being preceded by its dissimilar vowel *damna*, becomes و—as مائر becomes موثر. Whether the *alif-hamza* be the first, second, or final radical, the same rules of permutation are applicable.

---

* When the verb is concave in ی, then the servile و is cast out—thus مقیود becomes مقید.

## 25

| CONJ. | VERBAL NOUNS. | CONJ. | PARTICIPLES. |
|---|---|---|---|
| | اخرت, s.f. 'futurity;' from أخر. | 4th. | موكد, adj. 'confirmed,' 'corroborated;' from أكد. |
| 2nd. | تاخیر, s.f. 'delay,' 'procrastination;' from أخر. | 3rd. | ملایم, adj. 'gentle,' 'soft;' from لم. |
| ,, | تاکید, s.f. 'injunction;' from أكد. | 4th. | منشي, part. 'native instructor of languages,' 'moonshee;' from نشأ. |
| ,, | تاکید کرنا, v.a. 'enjoin strictly;' from أكد | | |
| ,, | تغذیه, s.m. 'food,' 'nourishment;' from غذأ. | 5th. | متاثر, adj. 'efficacious;' from أثر. |
| 4th. | انشا, s.f. 'writing,' 'composing;' from نشأ | 3rd. | موازي, adj. 'parallel;' from أزي. |
| 5th. | تغني, s.f. 'singing,' 'cooing;' from غنأ. | ,, | موانس, part. 'companion,' 'familiar;' from أنس. |
| 6th. | تلاش, s.f. 'investigation,' 'search;' from لاش. | 10th. | مستصال, adj. 'destroyed;' from أصل. |
| 8th. | امتلا, s.m. 'indigestion;' from ملأ. | | |
| 10th. | استصال, s.m. 'eradicating,' 'extirpating;' from أصل. | | |
| ,, | استرضا, s.m. 'seeking to please;' from رضأ. | | |

مثال, or Similar verbs, have their first radical either ي or و; their conjugations assimilate to the regular verb, partaking of fewer irregularities than the other imperfect verbs.

Those having و as وفق are more irregular than those which have ي as يسر. The regularly formed derivatives of these verbs are most generally used in Hindūstānī, as—

واقع, part. 'occurring;' from وقع.

موافق, part. 'according;' from وفق.

واسطي, s.m. 'on account of;' from وسط.

مواصلت, s. 'friendship;' from وصل.

ناقص, or Defective verbs, have و or ي for their last radical, as—غزا for غزو, and رضي for رضو. They are subject to various anomalies in their conjugations. There are a few derivatives of this description in Hindūstānī, as—

راضي, part. 'contented,' 'willing;' from رضا or رضو, s.f. 'permission,' 'leave,' and

رعيت, s.f. and m. 'cultivator,' 'tenant.'

رعايت, s.f. 'observance;' from رعي.

عادي, part. 'wicked,' 'transgressing;' from عدو.

عار or عاري, adj. 'naked,' 'modest;' from عري.

عاصي, adj. 'disobedient;' from عصي.

عافيت, s.f. 'health;' from عفو.

عالي, adj. 'high,' 'eminent;' from علو.

غازي, part. 'hew;' from غزا or غزو.

ملاقات, s.f. 'visit,' 'interview;' from لقو.

تماشا, s.m. 'a show.'

Besides these irregular verbs there are verbs which are defective and hamzated at the same time, as أدي; also doubly imperfect verbs, as وقي ; and concave and hamzated verbs, as أول. All the anomalies which occur in these verbs are founded on the same rules as the other irregular verbs; and, therefore, a further examination of them I think unnecessary.

## NOUNS.

The first class of nouns to be noticed are nouns of time, place, instrument or vessel. Nouns of time and place have م for their servile letter, as—مكتب, 'a school;' مجلس, 'time of sitting,' 'an assembly.' Nouns of place are, in some instances, distinguished from those of time by having *kasra* before their last radical, as—

مشرق, s.m. 'the east.'

مغرب, s.m. 'west.'

مطلع, s.m. 'the place of rising of the sun or stars,' 'east.'

مسكن, s.m. 'place of residence,' 'house.'

مسجد, s.m. 'a place of worship,' 'mosque.'

معركة, s.m. 'field of battle.'

Nouns derived from similar verbs, as وضع, make, for their nouns of time or place—

موضع, s.m. 'a village,' 'district.'

موطن, s.m. 'birth-place,' 'native country.'

ميعاد or موعد, s.m. 'time of promise,' 'foretelling.'

Concave verbs, as نوم, make—

مقام, s.m. 'an encamping ground,' 'halt.'  معاد, s.m. 'place of return, resurrection.'

مکان, s.m. 'place,' 'residence.'

Hamzated verbs, as لجا, make—

ملجا, s.m. 'asylum,' 'retreat.'  منشا, s.m. 'time of origin.'

Nouns of instrument and vessel may be distinguished from those of place by the servile م having *kasra*, as—

مِقَط, s.m. 'a piece of bone for nibbing reeds on; from قط.  مِقطع, s.m. 'shears,' 'cutting instrument.'

Nouns of instrument and vessel have likewise *alif* as a servile, as—

مِقراض, s.m. 'scissors,' 'shears.'  مِیزان, s.m. 'scales;' from وزن.

مِنقار, s.m. 'bird's bill.'

مِنقاش, s.m. 'pincers,' 'tweezers.'

The remaining class of nouns and adjectives to be noticed, are those which have ا, و, and ي, before their final radical, as—

| | |
|---|---|
| خلال, s.m. 'a tooth pick.' | خفیت, adj. 'light,' 'diminution of.' |
| حرام, s.m. 'forbidden.' | |
| لعاب, s.m. 'play,' 'saliva.' | حساب, s.f. 'accounts,' 'calculation.' |
| لسان, s.f. 'tongue.' | |
| عجاب, adj. 'wonderful.' | حفاظت, s.f. 'care,' 'watching.' |
| کرامت, s.f. 'excellence.' | |

عدول, s.m. 'deserting.'
قصور, s.m. 'fault.'
قبول, s.m. 'consent,' 'agree.'
حكيم, adj. 'doctor.' s.m. 'philosopher.'
حميل, s.m. 'a bastard,' 'surety.'
حميد, adj. 'praised.'
خصوص, s.m. 'especial;' from خص.
خصوصاً, adv. 'especially,' 'particularly.'
فضول, adj. 'excessive,' 'abundant.'
حريص, adj. 'greedy,' 'avaricious.'
سليم, s.m. 'perfect health, safety.'

اسم المنصوب, or the relative noun, is formed by adding ي to the different derivatives, as—

خلاصي, s.f. 'freedom.' s.m. 'a sailor.'
اعتراضي, s.f. 'opposition,' 'objection.'
ميراثي, adj. 'hereditary,' 'inherited.'
معشوقي, s.f. 'well-beloved,' 'mistress.'
عرضي, s.f. 'representation.'
فضولي, s.f. 'exuberance,' 'excess.'
قصوري, s.f. 'deficiency.'
اعتباري, adj. 'credit,' 'a confidant.'
حكيمي, s.f. 'practise of medicine.'
مضبوطي, s.f. 'strength,' 'firmness.'

And, again, some of these forms take the feminine ت, as—

معشوقيت, s.f. 'loveliness.'
معقوليت, s.f. 'reasonableness.'
معصوميت, s.f. 'innocence.'

## NUMBERS.

Nouns, in Arabic, have three numbers—singular, dual, and plural. The plural number is divided into regular (جمع سالم) and irregular or broken plurals (جمع مکسر); these plurals are subject to various anomalies, and have a variety of forms far too numerous to mention. The regular feminine plural is formed by adding ات, as—

| Plural. | | Plural. | |
|---|---|---|---|
| مشکلات | مشکلی, 'difficult.' | عورات | عور, 'a woman.' |
| معلومات | معلوم, 'known.' | تعمیرات | تعمیر, 'building.' |

In the forms of the broken plurals, some nouns have two and three plurals, as شاهد, 'a witness,'—plural, شواهد, انفاس, and ساهدون ; نفس, 'soul,' 'spirit,'—plural, شهود or نفوس.

The following are the forms of plurals which generally occur in Hindūstānī:—

| Plural. | | |
|---|---|---|
| اجسام | جسم, 'body.' | |
| احباب | حبب, 'friend.' | |
| احکام | حکم, 'command.' | |
| افلاک | فلک, 'heaven,' 'sky.' | |
| ارکان | رکن, 'pillar.' | |
| افواج | فوج, 'army.' | |
| افواه | فوه, 'mouth,' 'report.' | |
| اقوام | قوم, 'tribe.' | |
| عقول | عقل, 'science.' | |
| امور | امر, 'affair.' | |

| | Plural. |
|---|---|
| قلب, 'heart.' | قلوب |
| برج, 'bastion.' | بروج |
| غنير, 'strange.' | اغنيار |
| افق, 'horizon.' | افاق |
| غنيِ, 'rich.' | اغنيا |
| نبيِ, 'prophet.' | انبيا |
| عاشق, 'lover.' | عشاق |
| عادل, 'just.' | عدل |
| حاكم, 'governor.' | حكام |
| طريق, 'way.' | طرق or اطرق |
| كريم, 'noble.' | كرام |
| حكيم, 'physician.' | حكما |
| مال, 'property.' | اموال |
| وقت, 'time.' | اوقات |
| مدخل, 'a vestibule.' | مداخل |
| مسجد, 'a mosque.' | مساجد |

Beside the above plurals there are plurals of plurals, as—

| | 1st Pl. | 2nd Pl. |
|---|---|---|
| فرق | افراق | افاريق |
| ظفر | اظفار | اظافير |
| سوار | اسورت | اساور |

COMPARISON.

Under the head of comparison the Arabic nouns of diminution (اسم تصغير), excess (اسم مبالغه), and superiority

(اسم تفضيل), may be classed. The diminished noun, in words of three letters, is formed by taking ي before the last radical, as—صغر, 'small,' صغير, 'smaller;' رجل, 'a man,' رجيل, 'a little man:' and nouns of the form غلام, 'a boy,' make غليم, 'a little boy.' The nouns of excess take *alif*, as—وهب, 'liberal,' وهاب, 'most liberal;' علم, 'sciences,' علام, 'omniscient;' عطر, 'scent,' عطار, 'most scented,' 'a druggist.' The superlative noun takes *alif* as a prefix, as—

| | | | |
|---|---|---|---|
| حمق, 'foolish.' | | احمق, 'most foolish.' |
| حسن, 'handsome.' | | احسن, 'handsomer.' |
| شريف, 'noble.' | | اشرف, 'most noble.' |
| قصي, 'distant.' | | اقصي or اقصا, 'most distant,' 'extreme.' |
| كريم, 'merciful,' 'kind.' | | اكرام, 'most kind.' |
| كبير, 'great,' 'noble.' | | اكبر, 'most noble.' |

## TRILITERAL VERB.

Active Voice of كَتَبَ (= to write)

| Infinitive | Participle | Imperative | Future | Preterite | |
|---|---|---|---|---|---|
| كَتْبًا | كَاتِبٌ | اُكْتُبْ | يَكْتُبُ | كَتَبَ | 1 |
| تَكْتِيبًا | مُكَتِّبٌ | كَتِّبْ | يُكَتِّبُ | كَتَّبَ | 2 |
| مُكَاتَبًا | مُكَاتِبٌ | كَاتِبْ | يُكَاتِبُ | كَاتَبَ | 3 |
| إِكْتَابًا | مُكْتِبٌ | أَكْتِبْ | يُكْتِبُ | أَكْتَبَ | 4 |
| تَكَتُّبًا | مُتَكَتِّبٌ | تَكَتَّبْ | يَتَكَتَّبُ | تَكَتَّبَ | 5 |
| تَكَاتُبًا | مُتَكَاتِبٌ | تَكَاتَبْ | يَتَكَاتَبُ | تَكَاتَبَ | 6 |
| إِنْكِتَابًا | مُنْكَتِبٌ | إِنْكَتِبْ | يَنْكَتِبُ | إِنْكَتَبَ | 7 |
| إِكْتِتَابًا | مُكْتَتِبٌ | إِكْتَتِبْ | يَكْتَتِبُ | إِكْتَتَبَ | 8 |
| إِكْتِبَابًا | مُكْتَبٌّ | إِكْتَبِبْ | يَكْتَبُّ | إِكْتَبَّ | 9 |
| إِسْتِكْتَابًا | مُسْتَكْتِبٌ | إِسْتَكْتِبْ | يَسْتَكْتِبُ | إِسْتَكْتَبَ | 10 |
| إِكْتِيبَابًا | مُكْتَابٌّ | إِكْتَابِبْ | يَكْتَابُّ | إِكْتَابَّ | 11 |
| إِكْتِيتَابًا | مُكْتَوْتِبٌ | إِكْتَوْتِبْ | يَكْتَوْتِبُ | إِكْتَوْتَبَ | 12 |
| إِكْتِوَّابًا | مُكْتَوِّبٌ | إِكْتَوِّبْ | يَكْتَوِّبُ | إِكْتَوَّبَ | 13 |

## TRILITERAL VERB.

Passive *Voice of* كَتَبَ

| Participle. | Future. | Preterite. |    |
|-------------|---------|------------|----|
| مَكْتُوب     | يُكْتَبُ  | كُتِبَ      | 1  |
| مُكَتَّب     | يُكَتَّبُ | كُتِّبَ     | 2  |
| مُكَاتَب    | يُكَاتَبُ | كُوتِبَ    | 3  |
| مُكْتَب     | يُكْتَبُ  | أُكْتِبَ    | 4  |
| مُتَكَتَّب   | يُتَكَتَّبُ | تُكُتِّبَ   | 5  |
| مُتَكَاتَب  | يُتَكَاتَبُ | تُكُوتِبَ  | 6  |
| مُنْكَتَب   | يُنْكَتَبُ | أُنْكُتِبَ  | 7  |
| مُكْتَتَب   | يُكْتَتَبُ | أُكْتُتِبَ  | 8  |
| مُسْتَكْتَب | يُسْتَكْتَبُ | أُسْتُكْتِبَ | 10 |
| مُكْتَوْتَب | يُكْتَوْتَبُ | أُكْتُوتِبَ | 12 |
| مُكْتَوَّب  | يُكْتَوَّبُ | أُكْتُوِّبَ | 13 |

Printed by Libri Plureos GmbH in Hamburg,
Germany